IMPACT AML

*Let us catch it before the regulators do!*

# Independent Review for MSBs

# The Complete BSA/AML Audit Workbook

Howard Steiner
Stephen L. Marini

Independent Review for MSBs
The Complete BSA/AML Audit Workbook
Second Edition



ISBN-13: 978-0-6152-3992-7

**Published By**
**ImpactAML–INX3 Financial Press**
**Las Vegas, Nevada**

*Let us catch it before the regulators do!*

**Other Books by the Authors:**

SAR Investigations – The Complete BSA/AML Desktop Reference
Enhanced Due Diligence –The Complete BSA/AML Desktop Reference
Independent Review for Banks –The Complete BSA/AML Audit Workbook
Independent Review for Agents of MSBs –The Complete BSA/AML Audit Workbook
Risk Assessment for Tribal Casinos –The Complete BSA/AML Workbook

BSA/AML Training for MSBs – Unlimited Use Training Kit
The Risk Assessor™ Customer Risk Assessment Software
SAR and EDD Desktop Reference e-Books

## FORWARD

Money Service Businesses are required to conduct a formal risk assessment and periodically perform an independent review of their Bank Secrecy Act (BSA) compliance program. Some MSBs are complex operations, and the independent review requirement may best be carried out—at least in part—by an outside auditor. Other MSBs' operations are smaller, with simpler operations, and the review requirement may be conducted entirely by an MSB's own personnel. In either case, by using this NMTA endorsed Workbook, both types can save significant sums of money by performing much (or all) of their independent review by themselves.

The NMTA can also provide a review of your audit results and can assist you with drafting a custom BSA compliance program manual. Please see the NMTA website for further details (www.nmta.us) or contact the NMTA at:

> Phone: (516) 829-2742
> Form Mail: http://www.nmta.us/portal/contact.php

Keep in mind that our industry faces special challenges. It is essential to the future of our industry in general—and your business in particular!—that regulatory obligations are routinely fulfilled.

David Landsman
NMTA Executive Director

## HOW TO USE THIS WORKBOOK

- Each of the questions in this Workbook need to be answered in order to perform a complete and thorough review that will be sufficient for both your bank's and regulator's purposes.

- For the more complex questions, an explanation is provided immediately following the question. Each question should be answered by checking the appropriate yes or no box.

- The Comment section of each question should be filled out if you need to explain or qualify a yes or no answer, or add any other detail.

- You should use the *Follow-up* section of each question to make notes of actions you plan to take in the future, if need be, to address the comments you have recorded.

# Table of Contents

# Introduction

# Introduction

## The Review Process

Regulations do not require money services businesses to retain outside auditors to conduct the independent test of an anti-money laundering program. This is especially important for small money services businesses that may not have the ability to retain an outside auditing firm. FinCEN regulations require an independent review, *not a formal audit* by a certified public accountant or third-party consultant. Accordingly, a money services business does not necessarily need to hire an outside auditor or consultant. **The review may be conducted by an officer, employee or group of employees, so long as the reviewer is not the designated compliance officer and does not report directly to the compliance officer**. Even in instances when an MSB does employ the services of an outside consultant (lawyer, etc.), organizing–in advance–the information that the auditor will want to see will considerably lessen the time that auditor will need to complete his review. The costs an agent will incur for the auditor's service will likely be much less, as well.

The primary purpose of the independent review is to monitor the adequacy of you money services businesses' anti-money laundering program. The review should determine whether the business is operating in compliance with the requirements of the Bank Secrecy Act and your businesses' own policies and procedures. Each money services business should identify and assess the money laundering risks that may be associated with its unique products, services, customers, and geographic locations. Regardless of where risks arise, your money services business must take reasonable steps to manage them. Each money services business should focus resources on the areas of its business that management believes pose the greatest risks, and the level of sophistication of the associated internal controls should be appropriate for the size, structure, risks, and complexity of the money services business.

Your review must consider each requirement mandated by:

- ✓ The Bank Secrecy Act and PATRIOT Act
- ✓ Each State in which your MSB operates
- ✓ The Gramm-Leach-Bliley Act
- ✓ The Office of Foreign Assets Control (OFAC) provisions
- ✓ Your Licensee (or, Principal) under whose license you operate your MSB agency

From a high level, the Bank Secrecy Act / PATRIOT Act has four major requirements for money services businesses. These include:

- ✓ Implementation of written policies and procedures
- ✓ Designating an anti-money laundering compliance officer
- ✓ Providing training for appropriate personnel
- ✓ Providing for an independent review or audit of the compliance program

However, these four items contain many component parts. **These parts are collectively addressed by the individual questions in the sections of this Workbook.**

The best way to begin the review process is to first assemble all the documents your business has relating to the above requirements and then begin using this workbook. Each question in this workbook is very specific. Record your answers and any explanatory comments you might find necessary. (If you are in full compliance with a given question and can answer *YES*, then no comment may be needed. In cases where an item is not applicable to your business, you could, for example, use the Comments section to explain this.) For questions that you cannot immediately answer *YES* to, write down any follow-up tasks or action plan that you will take in order to be able to answer *YES* to these questions in the near future.

To complete your final review document, be sure to fill in the general business information in the next section.

**MSB Principals (Licensees)**

An MSB operating as a FinCEN registered money service business (Principal) whose business includes a network of agents (i.e., one or more agents) can still use this Guidebook as a template for its independent review. The Principal must complete the Agent List Section of the checklist. Still, operating an MSB with a network of agents may present certain business, operational, accounting and compliance risks that the operator may wish to address in addition to the review process provided here. If a registered Principal MSB is an owner/operator *without* a network of agents however, then this Guidebook's template should thoroughly suffice for BSA purposes.

## Money Services Business Defined

The term "money services business" includes any person doing business, whether or not on a regular basis or as an organized business concern, in one or more of the following capacities:

1. Currency dealer or exchanger
2. Check casher
3. Issuer of traveler's checks, money orders or stored value
4. Seller or redeemer of traveler's checks, money orders or stored value
5. Money transmitter
6. U.S. Postal Service

An activity threshold of greater than $1,000 per person per day in one or more transactions applies to the definitions of: currency dealer or exchanger; check casher; issuer of traveler's checks, money orders or stored value; and seller or redeemer of travelers' checks, money orders or stored value. The threshold applies separately to each activity -- if the threshold is not met for the specific activity, the person engaged in that activity is not an MSB on the basis of that activity.

No activity threshold applies to the definition of money transmitter. Thus, a person who engages as a business in the transfer of funds is an MSB as a money transmitter, regardless of the amount of money transmission activity.

Notwithstanding the previous discussion, the term "money services business" does not include:

- A bank, as that term is defined in 31 CFR 103.11(c); or,
- A person registered with, and regulated or examined by, the Securities and Exchange Commission or the Commodity Futures Trading Commission.

**Note:** For the complete regulatory definition of "money services business", see 31 C.F.R. 103.11(uu).

**Note:** Each money services business (MSB) is a financial institution. A "financial institution" includes any person doing business in one or more of the following capacities:

- Bank (except bank credit card systems)
- Broker or dealer in securities
- Money services business
- Telegraph company
- Casino
- Card club
- A person subject to supervision by any state or federal bank supervisory authority.

**Note:** For the regulatory definition of "financial institution," see 31 C.F.R. 103.11(n).

# Business Information

# Business Information

## Company Details

**FinCEN registered Principal and *no* agent network?: Yes___; No ___ (please check)**

**FinCEN registered Principal (i.e., *Licensee*) *with* a network of agents?: Yes___; No ___ (please check)**

**Agent only?: Yes___; No ___ (please check)**

**Business Name:** ______________________________

**Business Address:** ______________________________

______________________________

______________________________

**Business Phone #:** (   ) ____________________

**Business Fax #:** (   ) ____________________

**Business Tax ID #:** ______________________________

**e-Mail Address:** ______________________________

**Business Web site:** www.______________________________

**Business Owner:** ______________________________

**BSA Compliance Officer:** ______________________________

**Activities checked on FinCEN registration form, if applicable (for example, check casher, currency exchanger, etc.):**

______________________________

**Date of registration:** ______________________________

**Registration last renewed on date:** ______________________________

**States where the MSB operates and State licenses held (include all types):**

| STATE | DATE OF LICENSE | TYPE OF LICENSE (or reason why none is required) | RENEWAL DATE |
|---|---|---|---|
| | | | |
| | | | |
| | | | |
| | | | |
| | | | |
| | | | |
| | | | |
| | | | |
| | | | |

**Agent of what MSB Principal(s), *if applicable* (list all)?**

1. ______________________________
2. ______________________________
3. ______________________________
4. ______________________________
5. ______________________________
6. ______________________________

**Date of Agency Agreement:** ______________________________________

**Date of last independent or internal review:** __________________________

**Number of CTRs filed in last calendar year:** _________________________

**Number of SARs filed in last calendar year:** __________________________

**Last state regulatory exam date:** ___________________________________

**Date of corporate resolution formally adopting your AML Compliance Program:**

_____________________

**All corrective actions addressed from last exam? (circle one)**

___**Yes**

___ **No**

**Bank Account with:** ___________________________**Branch:**____________________

**Yearly transaction information:**

| MONTH | NUMBER OF REMITTANCES | TOTAL DOLLAR AMOUNT | AVERAGE VALUE OF REMITTANCES |
|---|---|---|---|
| JANUARY | | $ | $ |
| FEBRUARY | | $ | $ |
| MARCH | | $ | $ |
| APRIL | | $ | $ |
| MAY | | $ | $ |
| JUNE | | $ | $ |
| JULY | | $ | $ |
| AUGUST | | $ | $ |
| SEPTEMBER | | $ | $ |
| OCTOBER | | $ | $ |
| NOVEMBER | | $ | $ |
| DECEMBER | | $ | $ |

**Transaction information by geographic region:**

| COUNTRY | NUMBER OF REMITTANCES | TOTAL DOLLAR AMOUNT | AVERAGE VALUE OF REMITTANCES |
|---|---|---|---|
| | | $ | $ |
| | | $ | $ |
| | | $ | $ |
| | | $ | $ |
| | | $ | $ |
| | | $ | $ |
| | | $ | $ |

# Registered Principals

# Registered Principals
## Agent Listing

**NOTE: This section is to be completed only if MSB is a FinCEN registered MSB (with or without a network of agents)**

1. **Is a list of all of your MSB's Agents maintained by your MSB and does the list include the following information?** (Attach your agent list to this page)

| REQUIRED INFORMATION | Yes | No |
|---|---|---|
| The name of each Agent? | | |
| The address of each Agent? | | |
| Telephone number of each agent? | | |
| Type of services offered by each agent? | | |
| The year each agent became an agent of your MSB (after March 1, 2000)? | | |
| The number of branches or sub-branches for each agent (after March 1, 2000)? | | |
| Each Agent's gross transaction amount in the last 12 months where the amount exceeds $100,000? | | |
| Name and address of depository institution at which each Agent maintains an account for all or part of the funds received in or for the services the Agent provides on behalf of the MSB (whether the account is in the name of the Agent or the name of the MSB)? | | |

**Comments:**

**Follow-up:**

**2. Has your Agent List been revised as of each January 1 for the preceding 12 month period?**

☐ *Yes*

☐ *No*

**Comments:**

**Follow-up:**

**3. Has a copy of the initial agent list been retained for a period of 5 years?**

☐ *Yes*

☐ *No*

**Comments:**

**Follow-up:**

**4. Has a copy of each revised agent list been retained for five years?**

☐ *Yes*

☐ *No*

**Comments:**

**Follow-up:**

# AML Program

# AML Program

## Overview

FinCEN's regulations require money services businesses to establish anti-money laundering programs tailored to their operations and the risks posed. For example, the anti-money laundering program of a small money services business involved solely in the transmission of funds in small amounts will differ dramatically from the global money services business with both domestic and foreign agents.

Like other financial institutions subject to the Bank Secrecy Act, your money services businesses must develop and adopt written policies and procedures for compliance. You are also required to formally assess the risks of your business with respect to:

- The services the business offers;
- Your customer base;
- The markets you serve; and,
- The locations of your money services business.

Such information may be very simple for many small money services businesses operating in local areas with limited products, compared to, say, a sophisticated global money services business. Your AML program documentation must address each of the following:

✓ **Types of products and services offered by the money services business** –
- The categories of services engaged in by the particular money service business;
- Whether the money service business is a "principal" (with a fleet of agents) or an agent of another money services business;
- Whether or not money services represent a primary or ancillary aspect of the business (such as a grocery store that derives a small fraction of its overall revenue from cashing checks).

✓ **Location(s) and Market(s) served by the money services business:**
- The markets it targets;
- The locations it serves;
- Whether it offers international services; and,
- Whether it caters exclusively to local residents.

## Policy Statement

**1. Does your MSB have a written policy statement stating that:**

- ✓ **The company's policy is to fully comply with all legal an regulatory requirements for operating an MSB;**
- ✓ **All employees will be properly trained on an ongoing basis;**
- ✓ **Sufficient controls are in place to comply with legal and regulatory obligations; and**
- ✓ **Resources will be made available as needed to fulfill compliance obligations?**

(A policy statement should be included as part of your anti-money laundering compliance program documentation. It can be a simple document that states your businesses' intention to comply with the BSA and its regulations. The statement would include each of the items in the question above.)

☐ *Yes*

☐ *No*

**Comments:**

**Follow-up:**

# Compliance Program

1. **Do you have an up to date written compliance program, available for inspection upon request, that is tailored to its operations and the risks posed?**

   (MSBs are required to have a written anti-money laundering program. Even if you are an Agent for a Principal MSB, you must still have your own anti-money laundering compliance manual. While your bank is not required to request and maintain a copy of your AML program, it may choose to do so under certain circumstances. Your MSB is also required to formally assess the risks associated with it. These risks are described in the Risk Assessment section.)

   ☐ *Yes*

   ☐ *No*

**Comments:**

**Follow-up:**

**2. Is your AML compliance program accessible to all your employees?**

☐ *Yes*

☐ *No*

**Comments:**

**Follow-up:**

**3. Does your MSB's AML compliance program include policies and procedures that describe management's controls to prevent money laundering through your MSB?**

☐ *Yes*

☐ *No*

**Comments:**

**Follow-up:**

## Description of Management Controls

**1. Does your written anti-money laundering compliance program contain a description of management controls that are designed to ensure ongoing compliance?**

(Management controls are simply the policies and procedures used to reasonably ensure that the AML program achieves its intended results. The *intended results* are often defined and detailed by your Principal. In any case –at a minimum– they would include written procedures for training, recordkeeping, suspicious activity identification and reporting. Note: This question simply asks if your AML program documentation contains a "description" of these items.)

☐ *Yes*

☐ *No*

**Comments:**

**Follow-up:**

## Risk Assessment

1. **Has your MSB formally assessed the risks associated with:**
   - ✓ **the services it offers?**
   - ✓ **its customer base?**
   - ✓ **the markets it serves?**
   - ✓ **the locations of the money service business?**

   (A formal risk assessment is an exercise by which you analyze the above four items to judge the money laundering risks your business is exposed to. The results of your analysis should determine what specific steps (and the extent of the steps) you need to apply in order to meet your compliance obligations. For example, if a given risk is high, you might note in your compliance manual that on the basis of your risk analysis, a certain report is analyzed more frequently. Or, perhaps teller training for a specific type of risk (say, check fraud) is conducted more often. For this review's purposes, the question simply asks if you have already performed this step. If you have, it should have been documented in your compliance program documentation. For further information, see the Bank Risk Assessment Guidance in the Appendix.)

   ☐ *Yes*

   ☐ *No*

**Comments:**

**Follow-up:**

**2. Has your MSB taken reasonable steps to guard against money laundering and the financing of terrorism by assessing the risks and vulnerabilities associated with its operations?**

☐ *Yes*

☐ *No*

**Comments:**

**Follow-up:**

**3. Has your MSB taken reasonable steps to understand and comply with the requirements of the Bank Secrecy Act and applicable state laws?**

☐ *Yes*

☐ *No*

**Comments:**

**Follow-up:**

## Risks Posed by Location

1. **Does your anti-money laundering compliance program take into account the risks posed by the location of your business?**

   (This question is generally asking you if your written compliance program is risk-based with respect to your businesses' location. That is, if you:

   - ✓ have only one (or few) location(s) and provide services exclusively to local residents;
   - ✓ limit money transmitting activities to domestic entities (for example, domestic bill payments); and,
   - ✓ limit these activities to low dollar amounts…

   …then your AML program might not need to address the issues posed by, for example, MSBs that do send large sums internationally, or conduct large cash transactions with non-local residents. If your customers send money to others in countries considered at high risk for money laundering, drug related crimes, or terrorist activities, your compliance program should include the additional steps you are taking to ensure that these transactions are legitimate, and that suspicious activity training and detection procedures are described in the compliance program and are being followed.)

   ☐ *Yes*

   ☐ *No*

**Comments:**

**Follow-up:**

## Risks Posed by Size and Scope

1. **Does your anti-money laundering compliance program take into account the risks posed by the size and scope of your MSB's operations?**

   (The larger your operation, the more formally implemented and comprehensive your AML compliance program should be. The ***Size*** of your MSB's operation refers to:

   - The number of customers, number of transactions conducted; and,
   - Dollar volume of transactions conducted.

   ***Scope*** *of operations* refers to the:

   - Types of products and services offered;
   - Location your business serves (both domestically and internationally); and,
   - The domestic location of your business (for example, is your business located in a high intensity drug area?)

   ☐ *Yes*

   ☐ *No*

**Comments:**

**Follow-up:**

## Risks Posed by Volume and Nature of Financial Services Provided

1. **Does your anti-money laundering compliance program take into account the risks posed by the volume of the financial services provided?**

   (This question is similar to the previous question. If your MSB conducts large numbers of transactions, then your records and reports should sufficiently cover each product or service area and sufficient training should be a requirement of your AML program, especially where high volume and dollar products and/or services are involved.)

   ☐ *Yes*

   ☐ *No*

**Comments:**

**Follow-up:**

## Detection, Prevention and Reporting of Suspicious Activities

1. **Does your MSB's compliance program contain procedures that address the detection, reporting, and prevention of money laundering related activity?**

   (MSBs are required to file Currency Transaction Reports and Suspicious Activity Reports in certain situations. These should be addressed in the written compliance program.)

   ☐ *Yes*

   ☐ *No*

**Comments:**

**Follow-up:**

## Verifying Customer Identification

1. **Does your MSB's compliance program address customer verification requirements?**

   (MSBs are required to verify the identity of customers sending $3,000 or more. The sender must be able to reliably establish his/her identity and address. If the sender is sending funds for a third party, both the sender and the third party are required to provide identification. The compliance program should address the topic of customer verification.)

   ☐ *Yes*

   ☐ *No*

**Comments:**

**Follow-up:**

# Filing Required Reports

1. **Does your MSB's compliance program address filing of CTRs and SARs?**

   (MSBs are required to file CTRs and in some cases, must file SARs. The compliance program must address these topics.)

   ☐ *Yes*

   ☐ *No*

**Comments:**

**Follow-up:**

## Creating and Retaining Records

1. **Does your MSB's compliance program include policies, procedures, and internal controls associated with creating and retaining records?**

   (Records must be kept for a period of five years from the date of their creation. The definition of records is very broad and includes items such as compliance manuals. training logs, identification verifications, customer receipts, reports (such as CTRs and SARs), management documents (such as those provided to you by your Licensee), regulatory communications, etc.)

   ☐ *Yes*

   ☐ *No*

**Comments:**

**Follow-up:**

## Responding to Law Enforcement Requests

1. **Does your written compliance program include a procedure describing how your MSB is to respond to law enforcement requests and keep such inquiries confidential?**

   (There are different types of requests you may receive from law enforcement agencies such as the IRS or FBI. There are also confidentiality requirements that should be part of your documentation as well as presented during the training you give to employees.)

   ☐ *Yes*

   ☐ *No*

**Comments:**

**Follow-up:**

## Referencing Automated Systems

1. **If your MSB uses automated systems for transaction monitoring, reporting, training, etc., are there descriptive references to these in your written compliance program?**

   (Systems used to fulfill compliance tasks should be described in your compliance procedures within your AML compliance manual.)

   ☐ *Yes*

   ☐ *No*

**Comments:**

**Follow-up:**

# Compliance Officer

# Compliance Officer

## Compliance Officer Designation

1. **Is there a designated compliance officer for your MSB and is this person's name noted in your compliance documentation or manual?**

   (MSBs are required to designate a compliance officer to implement the anti-money laundering program and implement the tasks required of the program. The individual holding this position is not required to devote full time to this position, but may hold other jobs in your business as well.)

   ☐ *Yes*

   ☐ *No*

**Comments:**

**Follow-up:**

**2. Is the designated compliance officer for your MSB sufficiently trained and knowledgeable to carry out the tasks of the job an reasonably prevent money laundering activities through your MSB**

(Compliance officer training should be documented and retained. Training can be evidenced by certificates of training seminars attended, courses taken, professional certifications, etc. )

☐ *Yes*

☐ *No*

**Comments:**

**Follow-up:**

# Compliance Officer Duties

1. **Does your compliance manual or other AML compliance documentation specifically assign to the designated compliance officer or his designee the task of ensuring that all regulatory reports are filed in a complete and timely fashion?**

   (Your AML program documentation should state who the compliance officer is and include the duties that the compliance officer is responsible for. Where the compliance officer is delegating certain tasks to other employees, those employees' names and their assigned tasks should be stated in the compliance manual as well.)

   ☐ *Yes*

   ☐ *No*

**Comments:**

**Follow-up:**

**2. Does your compliance manual or other AML compliance documentation specifically assign to the designated compliance officer or his designee the task of providing AML training recordkeeping of all the training conducted?**

☐ *Yes*

☐ *No*

**Comments:**

**Follow-up:**

3. **Does your compliance manual or other AML compliance documentation assign to the designated compliance officer or his designee the task of providing specific training to employees regarding the detection and reporting of suspicious activities or transactions?**

☐ *Yes*

☐ *No*

**Comments:**

**Follow-up:**

**4. Does your compliance manual or other AML compliance documentation specifically assign to the designated compliance officer or his designee the task of scheduling independent periodic compliance reviews?**

☐ *Yes*

☐ *No*

**Comments:**

**Follow-up:**

**5. Does your compliance manual or other AML compliance documentation specifically assign to the designated compliance officer or his designee the task of making all employees aware of the AML compliance program?**

☐ *Yes*

☐ *No*

**Comments:**

**Follow-up:**

**6. Does your compliance manual or other AML compliance documentation specifically assign to the designated compliance officer or his designee the task of providing for transaction monitoring to detect structuring activity or other money laundering activity?**

(Your compliance program should describe who is responsible for monitoring, how often and by what procedures transactions are monitored, and also include sample red flags that are indicative of suspicious activity.)

☐ *Yes*

☐ *No*

**Comments:**

**Follow-up:**

# Training Program

# Training Program

## Personnel Requiring Training

1. **Is training provided for all compliance staff as well as officers, directors and employees?**

   (Training for compliance staff, officers and directors should be comprehensive in scope. Training for employees should also be specific to the job duties performed. For example, tellers should be especially knowledgeable on topics related to suspicious activity identification and cash transaction requirements.)

   ☐ *Yes*

   ☐ *No*

**Comments:**

**Follow-up:**

**2. Are your firm's training policies sufficient regarding scope and frequency of training such that they demonstrate the importance management places in ongoing education and training?**

(Banks and regulators need to see proof that the senior management of your business takes its BSA obligations seriously. Providing detailed training at regular intervals to all appropriate managers and employees would constitute such proof. It is important that you can document that the training has taken place. A simple training log can provide such proof. The training material should also be available for inspection by regulators or your banker as proof of the scope of training.)

☐ *Yes*

☐ *No*

**Comments:**

**Follow-up:**

**3. Are newly hired employees trained prior to beginning their work assignments?**

(New hires should be trained before starting their work assignments. All employees should be completely familiar with your firm's compliance program.)

☐ *Yes*

☐ *No*

**Comments:**

**Follow-up:**

## Ongoing Training

1. **Does each employee receive training on a recurring basis that includes updates when new laws or regulations are issued?**

   (Training should be refreshed at least annually. The training program should also provide for updated training on an as-needed basis when new laws, regulations, or company policies are issued that require updating employees training.)

   ☐ *Yes*

   ☐ *No*

**Comments:**

**Follow-up:**

## Large Currency Transactions

**1. Does your MSB's training program provide specific information related the reporting of large cash transactions?**

(This training should include information pertaining to the need to file Cash Transaction Reports (CTRs) forms, how to fill out the form, and the procedure for how the CTR form gets filed by your MSB.)

☐ ***Yes***

☐ ***No***

**Comments:**

**Follow-up:**

**2. Are your employees alert for activities related to customers who might *structure* transactions to avoid the $10,000 reporting limit?**

(Customers may try to avoid the CTR reporting limit by breaking large transactions into smaller parts. Employees should be trained to recognize the red flags for such customer activity. Additionally, employees should take care not to advise or assist customers in any way regarding structuring of transactions.)

☐ *Yes*

☐ *No*

**Comments:**

**Follow-up:**

## Suspicious Activity Reporting

1. **Does your MSB's training program provide specific information related the reporting of suspicious activities or alleged criminal conduct?**

   (This training should include information pertaining to Suspicious Activity Reports (SAR-MSB) forms and USA PATRIOT Act Section 314b provisions for voluntarily filing SARs on activities that might not be reportable because of the thresholds, but nonetheless are still suspicious. Reporting to local law enforcement should also be covered.)

   ☐ *Yes*

   ☐ *No*

**Comments:**

**Follow-up:**

**2. Do policies and training dictate when and how an employee should report observed suspicious activity to his/her manager or to the MSB compliance officer?**

☐ *Yes*

☐ *No*

**Comments:**

**Follow-up:**

# Record Retention

1. **Does your MSB's training program provide specific information related to the requirements for record retention?**

   (This training should include information pertaining to record retention for both Cash Transaction Reports (CTRs) forms.)

   ☐ *Yes*

   ☐ *No*

**Comments:**

**Follow-up:**

## Sales and Purchases of Monetary instruments

1. **Does your training program specifically cover sales and purchases of monetary instruments and their requirements?**

☐ *Yes*

☐ *No*

**Comments:**

**Follow-up:**

## Money Laundering Methods

1. **Does your MSB's program for educating appropriate employees regarding the Bank Secrecy Act (BSA) cover examples of money laundering cases and the methods in which activities can be detected/resolved/reported?**

   ☐ *Yes*

   ☐ *No*

**Comments:**

**Follow-up:**

## Forms of Money Laundering

1. **Does your MSB's program for educating appropriate employees regarding the BSA cover an overview of the different forms that money laundering can take (deposit accounts, wire transfer loans, etc.)?**

☐ *Yes*

☐ *No*

**Comments:**

**Follow-up:**

# Funds Transfer Activity

1. **Does your MSB's program for educating appropriate employees regarding the BSA cover wire (fund) transfer activity?**

   ☐ *Yes*

   ☐ *No*

**Comments:**

**Follow-up:**

# OFAC Training

1. **Does your MSB's program for educating appropriate employees cover OFAC requirements?**

☐ *Yes*

☐ *No*

**Comments:**

**Follow-up:**

## SAR Disclosure

1. **Do your MSB's policies, procedures and training specifically cover the prohibition from disclosing to a person involved in a transaction that a suspicious activity report has been filed?**

☐ *Yes*

☐ *No*

**Comments:**

**Follow-up:**

**2. Does your MSB's training address the situation where a person who is subpoenaed or asked to disclose a SAR (other than by FinCEN or a regulatory or law enforcement agency) shall decline to produce the SAR and shall notify FinCEN of the request?**

☐ *Yes*

☐ *No*

**Comments:**

**Follow-up:**

# Independent Audit & Testing

# Independent Audit & Testing

## Review Process

1. **Does your independent review process include testing of internal controls and transactional systems and procedures to identify problems and weaknesses and, if necessary, recommend to management appropriate corrective actions?**

   (Testing can encompass many different things. Quizzing employees periodically on their AML knowledge and duties can be one sort of test. Periodically examining reports and logs that are the responsibility of others can be another type of control test. Testing should include a review to ensure that all reportable cash transactions have been the subject of a CTR and have been properly filed or mailed to the government. Testing should be addressed in your AML procedures compliance manual.)

   ☐ *Yes*

   ☐ *No*

**Comments:**

**Follow-up:**

## Documenting the Scope of the Review

**2. Has the person or persons responsible for conducting the independent review documented the scope of the review, procedures performed, transaction testing completed, if any, and the findings of the review?**

(Without documented evidence of the review, a regulatory examiner or your bank will simply assume that the review was either not conducted or was not sufficient in scope. Documented reviews should be maintained with your records for at least five years. Documentation of reviews need to be accessible to government examiners and law enforcement personnel who have authority to examine such documents.)

☐ *Yes*

☐ *No*

**Comments:**

**Follow-up:**

**3. Have recommendations to management for corrective actions, if any, been documented and retained?**

☐ *Yes*

☐ *No*

**Comments:**

**Follow-up:**

# Registration

# Registration

## Overview

With few exceptions, each money services business (MSB) must register with the Department of the Treasury. A person that is an MSB solely because that person serves as an agent of another MSB is not required to register.

**Exceptions:**

**1. Solely an Agent** - A person that is an MSB solely because that person serves as an agent of another MSB is not required to register. However, a person that is an MSB *both* because it engages in MSB activities on its own behalf *and* as an agent of another MSB, must register. (A person (defined by 31 C.F.R. 103.11 (z), is an individual, a corporation, a partnership, a trust or estate, a joint stock company, an association, a syndicate, joint venture, or other unincorporated organization or group, an Indian Tribe (as that term is defined in the Indian Gaming Regulatory Act), and all entities cognizable as legal personalities.)

A person that is an MSB solely because that person serves as an agent of another MSB is not required to register. However, a person that is an MSB both because it engages in MSB activities on its own behalf and as an agent of another MSB must register. Federal guidance provides the following example regarding agent status and registration:

- A supermarket corporation that acts as an agent (as a seller of money orders) for an issuer of money orders, and performs no other services of a nature and amount that would cause the supermarket corporation to be a money services business, is not required to register. The result is the same if the supermarket corporation serves as an agent for two or more MSBs. Thus, if the supermarket corporation serves as an agent both of a money order issuer and of a money transmitter, it is not required to register. However, registration is required if the supermarket corporation --in addition to acting as an agent of a money order issuer --cashed checks or exchanged currency (other than as an agent for another MSB) in an amount greater than $1,000 for any person on any day in one or more transactions. 31 CFR 103.41(a)(2)

**2. Stored value** - Funds or monetary value represented in digital electronics format (whether or not specially encrypted) and stored or capable of storage on electronic media in such a way as to be retrievable and transferable electronically. 31 C.F.R. 103.11(vv) - A person that is an MSB solely as an issuer, seller, or redeemer of stored value is not required to register. However, a person that is an MSB as an issuer, seller, or redeemer of stored value and engages in MSB activities (of a nature and value that cause the person to be an MSB on a basis other than stored value) must register.

**3. U.S. Postal Service, Government Agencies** - Agencies of the United States, of any State, or of any political subdivision of any State.

Registration of an MSB is the responsibility of the owner or controlling person of the MSB.

**Owner or Controlling Person** - An owner or controlling person includes the following:

| MSB | Owner or Controlling Person |
|---|---|
| Sole Proprietorship | The individual who owns the business |
| Partnership | A general partner |
| Trust | A trustee |
| Corporation | The largest single shareholder |

- If the MSB is a public corporation, a duly authorized officer of the public corporation may register the MSB and may sign the form on behalf of the corporation.
- If two or more persons own equal numbers of shares of an MSB that is a corporation, those persons may enter into an agreement designating one of them to register the MSB.
- If the owner or controlling person is a corporation, a duly authorized officer of the owner-corporation may sign the form on behalf of the owner-corporation.

**Registration Renewals**

The registration of each MSB must be renewed every 2 years. At the end of the initial registration period of two years, an updated registration form must be filed.

A copy of the filed registration form and other supporting documentation must be retained at a location in the United States for a period of five years. That information includes:

1. A copy of the filed registration form;
2. Estimate of Business Volume - Estimate of the business volume of the MSB for the coming year;
3. Ownership or Control - Information with regard to the ownership or control of the MSB;
4. Agent List - A listing of agents that the MSB has authorized to sell or distribute its MSB services.

**Re-registration**

Re-register means to re-file a registration form (with information different from that reported on the form originally filed) during the initial registration period (before the deadline for renewal) because an event triggering re-registration has occurred. An MSB must be re-registered when any of the following events occurs during a registration period:

- Change in Ownership or Control under State Law - There has been a change in ownership or control of the MSB that requires the MSB to be re-registered under State law;
- Transfer of Voting Power or Equity Interest - More than 10 percent of the voting power or equity interest of the MSB has been transferred (except MSBs that must report such transfer to the Securities and Exchange Commission);
- Increase in the Number of Agents - The number of agents of the MSB has increased by more than 50 percent.

To re-register, the registration form, TD F 90-22.55, must be completed and filed not later than 180 days after the date the triggering event occurs.

The calendar year in which the triggering event occurs is treated as the first year of a new 2-year registration period. 31 CFR 103.41(b)(4)

## Registration Filing (Agents may skip to the last question)

1. **Has your MSB registered with the Department of the Treasury and filed FinCEN Form 107 Registration of Money Services Business?** (Applicable only for Principal MSBs, *not* Agents.)

   (Care should be taken to ensure that the activities indicated on the registration form include all the activities your MSB engages in. Updates to the filing should be made when activities are added or removed from your MSB's operation.)

   ☐ *Yes*

   ☐ *No*

**Comments:**

**Follow-up:**

**2. Has your MSB registered, as required, with the Department of the Treasury and filed *FinCEN Form 107 Registration of Money Services Business* within a 180-day period beginning on the day following the date your business was established?** (Applicable only for Principal MSBs, *not* Agents.)

☐ *Yes*

☐ *No*

**Comments:**

**Follow-up:**

3. **Has an updated registration form been filed every two years by December 31st at the end of the two-calendar year period, as required, following the initial registration?** (Applicable only for Principal MSBs, *not* Agents.)

   ☐ *Yes*

   ☐ *No*

**Comments:**

**Follow-up:**

4. **Have any of the events listed below –triggering re-registration, occurred since the last registration filing and if so, has re-registration been submitted**? (Applicable only for Principal MSBs, *not* Agents.)
   - ✓ **Change in ownership or control under state law?**
   - ✓ **Transfer of 10% or more of the voting power or equity interest?**
   - ✓ **An increase in the number of agents exceeding 50%?**

   ☐ *Yes*

   ☐ *No*

**Comments:**

**Follow-up:**

5. **If an event triggered a change, has FinCEN Form 107 (formerly) *TD F 90-22.55* been completed and filed not later than 180 days after the date the triggering event occurs**? (Applicable only for Principal MSBs, *not* Agents.)

☐ ***Yes***

☐ ***No***

**Comments:**

**Follow-up:**

**6. Has a copy of your MSB's filed registration form been retained at a location in the United States for a period of five years at a location in the United States?** (Applicable only for Principal MSBs, *not* Agents.)

☐ *Yes*

☐ *No*

**Comments:**

**Follow-up:**

7. **Has other supporting documentation, listed below and relevant to registration, been retained for five years at a location in the United States?** (Applicable only for Principal MSBs, *not* Agents.)

- ✓ **A copy of the filed registration form?**
- ✓ **Estimate of the business volume of the MSB for the coming year?**
- ✓ **Information with regard to the ownership or control of the MSB?**
- ✓ **A listing of agents that the MSB has authorized to sell or distribute its MSB services?**

☐ *Yes*

☐ *No*

**Comments:**

**Follow-up:**

**8. Has the location referred to in the question above been reported on the registration form and reflect either the address of your MSB reported on the Form (in Part I, Registrant Information) or another address reported on the Form (in Part V, Location of Supporting Documentation)?** (Applicable only for Principal MSBs, *not* Agents.)

☐ *Yes*

☐ *No*

**Comments:**

**Follow-up:**

**9. Has your MSB complied with all applicable *state* licensing requirements and are the registration documents for each state available for inspection by your bank or regulatory agency?**

☐ *Yes*

☐ *No*

**Comments:**

**Follow-up:**

# Currency Exchange Records

# Currency Exchange Records

## Recording Transactions

1. **For each currency exchange (either foreign or domestic), either in or out, in excess of $1,000, is a record created capturing the customer's ID and transaction information?**

   ☐ *Yes*

   ☐ *No*

**Comments:**

**Follow-up:**

**2. For each currency exchange (either foreign or domestic) in or out in excess of $1,000, are the records created retained for five years from the date of each transaction?**

☐ *Yes*

☐ *No*

**Comments:**

**Follow-up:**

# Currency Transaction Reporting

# Currency Transaction Reporting

## CTR Filing

1. **Does your MSB file a report of each currency transaction involving cash-in or cash-out of more than $10,000 conducted by or through the MSB on any one day by or on behalf of the same person?**

☐ *Yes*

☐ *No*

**Comments:**

**Follow-up:**

**2. Are CTR forms filed within 15 days from the date of the transaction(s), as required?**

(You should maintain a log of CTRs that included the date mailed.)

☐ *Yes*

☐ *No*

**Comments:**

**Follow-up:**

**3. For each CTR, does your MSB verify and record the customer's ID?**

☐ *Yes*

☐ *No*

**Comments:**

**Follow-up:**

**4. For each CTR, does your MSB obtain transaction information?**

☐ *Yes*

☐ *No*

**Comments:**

**Follow-up:**

**5. For each CTR, does your MSB keep a copy for 5 years from the date of filing the report?**

☐ *Yes*

☐ *No*

**Comments:**

**Follow-up:**

## Aggregation of Transactions

1. **For aggregation purposes, are *cash-in* transactions added together with *cash-out* transactions to determine whether the CTR threshold (greater than $10,000) has been met in any one business day?**

   (If you are aware that a series of transactions originated from a single source within a single day, you must aggregate those transactions to determine the necessity of filing a CTR. Transactions that originate from a single source over several days may still potentially be an attempt to structure the transactions to avoid the reporting limit. However, because the transactions do not have to be aggregated over a period of days, no CTR would be required, but a SAR filing may indeed be warranted.)

   ☐ *Yes*

   ☐ *No*

**Comments:**

**Follow-up:**

# Suspicious Activity Reporting

# Suspicious Activity Reporting

## Overview

Certain money services businesses (MSB) are required to report suspicious activity. The following MSBs are subject to the suspicious activity reporting (SAR) requirement:

- ✓ Money transmitters
- ✓ Currency Dealers or Exchangers
- ✓ Money order - issuers, sellers or redeemers
- ✓ Traveler's check - issuers, sellers or redeemers
- ✓ US Postal Service

A report must be filed when a transaction that is conducted by, at or through the MSB is both a) suspicious, and b) $2,000 or more.

An MSB must file a Suspicious Activity Report (SAR) when a transaction is greater than $2,000 under the following circumstances:

- ✓ Involves funds derived from illegal activity or is intended or conducted in order to hide or disguise funds or assets derived from illegal activity, or is...
- ✓ Designed to evade the requirements of the Bank Secrecy Act, whether through structuring or other means, or...
- ✓ Serves no business or apparent lawful purpose, and the reporting business knows of no reasonable explanation for the transaction after examining all available facts, or...
- ✓ Involves use of the money services business to facilitate criminal activity.

Where a transaction is suspicious but falls under the threshold, or where the activity is exempt from reporting (such as check cashing), the MSB may still *voluntarily* file a SAR.

The MSB must file the SAR no later than 30 days after the determination was made that the transaction was in fact suspicious. In no case should the time between the transaction and the filing exceed 60 days. The SAR forms must be sent to:

Detroit Computing Center, ATTN: SAR-MSB,
P.O. Box 33117
Detroit MI 48232-5980.

In situations involving violations that require immediate attention, such as ongoing money laundering schemes, the MSB is to notify the appropriate law enforcement authority immediately, by telephone, in addition to filing the required form.

A copy of the filed form and supporting documentation must be retained for a period of five years from the date of filing. Supporting documentation and a copy of the filed form must be retained by the MSB for a period of five years from the date of the filing of the SAR. Supporting documentation includes relevant business records such as copies of instruments; copies of money transfer forms; receipts; sale, transaction or clearance records, and photographs, surveillance audio and/or video recording medium. Originals or the business record equivalent must be kept with a copy of the filed SAR.

MSBs (including any director, officer, or employee of MSBs) are prohibited from disclosing to a person involved in the transaction that a Suspicious Activity Report (SAR) has been filed. The disclosure prohibition includes providing any information that would disclose that a SAR has been filed. A person who is subpoenaed or asked to disclose a SAR (other than by FinCEN or a regulatory or law enforcement agency) shall decline to produce the SAR and shall notify FinCEN of the request

## Reported Transactions

1. **Have suspicious activity reports been filed for transactions that have been conducted by, at, or through the MSB and that are both suspicious and in the amount of $2,000 or greater ($5,000 or more for issuers reviewing clearance records)?**

   (Copies of the reports should exist in a secure location along with a log showing the dates these were filed with the government.)

   ☐ *Yes*

   ☐ *No*

**Comments:**

**Follow-up:**

**2. Have transactions been reported where your MSB suspected that a transaction involves funds derived from illegal activity or is intended or conducted in order to hide or disguise funds or assets derived from illegal activity?**

☐ *Yes*

☐ *No*

**Comments:**

**Follow-up:**

**3. Have transactions been reported where the MSB suspects that a transaction involves activity designed to evade the requirements of the Bank Secrecy Act, whether through structuring or other means?**

☐ *Yes*

☐ *No*

**Comments:**

**Follow-up:**

**4. Have transactions been reported where the MSB suspects that a transaction serves no business or apparent lawful purpose, and the reporting business knows of no reasonable explanation for the transaction after examining all available facts?**

- ☐ *Yes*
- ☐ *No*

**Comments:**

**Follow-up:**

**5. Have transactions been reported where the MSB suspects that a transaction involves use of the money services business to facilitate criminal activity?**

☐ *Yes*

☐ *No*

**Comments:**

**Follow-up:**

**6. When SARs have been filed, has the proper form –Suspicious Activity Report by Money Services Business (SAR-MSB), been utilized?**

☐ *Yes*

☐ *No*

**Comments:**

**Follow-up:**

7. **When SARs have been filed, did the narrative section completely, clearly, and accurately describe the nature and circumstances of the suspicious activity?**

☐ *Yes*

☐ *No*

**Comments:**

**Follow-up:**

**8. Has your MSB filed the required MSB SAR Form no later than 30 calendar days after the date of the initial detection by the MSB of facts that the MSB knows, suspects or has reason to suspect the transaction may be suspicious?**

☐ *Yes*

☐ *No*

**Comments:**

**Follow-up:**

# Monetary Instruments Log

# Monetary Instruments Log

## Overview

If your MSB sells money orders, traveler's checks, or other instruments above $3,000 for cash, you must verify the identity of customers purchasing these, and create and maintain a record of each purchase.

For amounts between $3,000 and $10,000 inclusive, you must also record:

- ✓ The amount of the transaction
- ✓ The serial numbers of the instruments, and…
- ✓ The date of the transaction

## Recording Transactions

**1. If your MSB sells money orders, traveler's checks, or other instruments for cash does it verify the identity of the customers and create and maintain a record of each purchase?**

☐ *Yes*

☐ *No*

**Comments:**

**Follow-up:**

2. **If your MSB sells money orders, traveler's checks, or other instruments for cash involving amounts between $3,000 and $10,000 inclusive, does it create and maintain a record of each purchase including the amount of the transaction, the serial numbers of the instruments, and the date sold?**

☐ *Yes*

☐ *No*

**Comments:**

**Follow-up:**

**3. For each record, does your MSB keep a copy for 5 years from the date of the transaction?**

☐ *Yes*

☐ *No*

**Comments:**

**Follow-up:**

# Funds Transfer

# Funds Transfer

## Verification of Identity

1. **When your MSB accepts an instruction to send a money transfer of $3,000 or more, does it verify the identity of the *send* customer?**

   (A policy statement should exist in your AML program documentation, and a detailed procedure should exist in your compliance manual. Training materials should also address this requirement. A log or other evidence should exist for each transaction to support that this requirement is fulfilled for each qualifying transaction.)

   ☐ *Yes*

   ☐ *No*

**Comments:**

**Follow-up:**

**2. When your MSB accepts an instruction to pay a money transfer of $3,000 or more does it verify the identity of the *receiving* customer?**

(See explanatory comment above.)

☐ *Yes*

☐ *No*

**Comments:**

| |
|---|
| |

**Follow-up:**

| |
|---|
| |

## Recording Funds Transfer Transactions

1. **When your MSB accepts an instruction to send a money transfer of $3,000 or more, does it create and maintain a record of the money transfer, regardless of the method of payment?**

   (A policy statement should exist in your AML program documentation, and a detailed procedure should exist in your compliance manual. Training materials should also address this requirement. A log or other evidence should exist for each transaction to support that this requirement is fulfilled for each qualifying transaction.)

   ☐ *Yes*

   ☐ *No*

**Comments:**

**Follow-up:**

**2. When your MSB accepts an instruction to pay a money transfer of $3,000 or does it create a record of the money transfer, regardless of the method of payment?**

(See explanatory comment for Question #1.)

☐ *Yes*

☐ *No*

**Comments:**

**Follow-up:**

**3. When your MSB accepts an instruction to pay a money transfer of $3,000 or does it maintain a record of the money transfer regardless of the method of payment, for a period of 5 years from the date of the transaction?**

☐ *Yes*

☐ *No*

**Comments:**

**Follow-up:**

# OFAC

# OFAC

## Overview

OFAC is the law enforcement agency that administers economic and trade sanctions against targeted countries, terrorists, international drug traffickers, and those engaged in the proliferation of weapons of mass destruction.

OFAC publishes:

- ✓ A list of countries that American firms are prohibited from conducting business with.
- ✓ A list of persons and entities who are prohibited from transacting any business in America through American firms, or with American citizens.

Penalties for non-compliance have ranged from $11,000 all the way up to $1 million per transaction, and include possible criminal prosecution.

Your OFAC compliance program is most likely tied in closely with your Principal, who would normally scan transactions against the OFAC published list. However, there are still requirements regarding *rejecting* transactions at point of sale, and training (as noted in the question pertaining to OFAC in the Training Section of the Checklist), that need to be fulfilled at a minimum.

## Rejecting and Reporting Transactions

**1. Does your MSB have systems in place to match customer names against the OFAC list at the teller window?**

- ☐ *Yes*
- ☐ *No*

**Comments:**

**Follow-up:**

**2. Have tellers received sufficient training to handle events when a customer's name registers a positive match to the OFAC list?**

☐ *Yes*

☐ *No*

**Comments:**

**Follow-up:**

# State Requirements

# State Requirements

## Overview

Most states have licensing and other requirements with which your money services business must comply. These requirements can differ markedly from state to state, and can include items that the federal Bank Secrecy regulations do not even touch upon. Such requirements can include:

- ✓ Bond, or in lieu thereof, minimum Bonded/Letter of Credit/Deposit;
- ✓ Minimum net worth requirements depending on number of locations;
- ✓ Proof of sound financial condition;
- ✓ Current status for payment of status and fees;
- ✓ "Muster" background checks;
- ✓ Business plans;
- ✓ Contracts if utilizing authorized delegates:
    - Certification form delegates that they understand MSB statutes;
    - Outline records;
    - Acknowledgement of receipt of procedures;
    - Notice to agent that it is subject to state banking department examination.
- ✓ Periodic (e.g., quarterly) report filing for:
    - Transaction volume limits; and,
    - Financial statements.
- ✓ Permissible investments;
- ✓ Transaction receipt disclosures;
- ✓ Consumer compliant notice postings;
- ✓ Annual license renewal and assessment fees;
- ✓ Annual registration renewal applications.

**NOTE: It is extremely important for you to know and comply with these laws.**

**<u>WHERE TO FIND STATE RELEATED INFORMATION</u>**

The website www.msb.gov has a list of each states' regulatory agency and detailed contact information. The list can be found at this url:

http://www.msb.gov/pdf/msbstatecontactsfinal.pdf

## State Audit Questions

1. **Has your MSB documented all the requirements related to state regulations for each and every state in which it operates?**

   (Since each state has differing laws regulating MSBs, it absolutely necessary to attain all the information regarding regulatory requirements from each state in which your MSB operates.)

   ☐ *Yes*

   ☐ *No*

**Comments:**

**Follow-up:**

**2. Has your MSB documented all the requirements related to state regulations for each and every state in which it operates?**

(Since each state has differing laws regulating MSBs, it absolutely necessary to attain all the information regarding regulatory requirements from each state in which your MSB operates.)

☐ *Yes*

☐ *No*

**Comments:**

**Follow-up:**

# Gramm-Leach-Bliley Act

# Gramm-Leach-Bliley Act

## Privacy Policies and Procedures

1. **Does your AML compliance program specifically address the requirements of the Gramm-Leach-Bliley Act (GLB)?**

   (GLB mandates that your MSB protect your clients' personal information. Notices of privacy protection provided to customers, and procedures that address safeguarding client data and records may be sufficient to prove compliance with GLB. Your compliance manual, policies, procedures, etc. should specifically address the requirements of this important Act.)

   ☐ *Yes*

   ☐ *No*

**Comments:**

**Follow-up:**

# Company Compliance

# Company Compliance

## Internal Policies, Procedures and Directives

1. **Are the policies of your parent company (Licensee) fully incorporated into your MSB's anti-money laundering compliance program?**

   (Besides being a legal contractual requirement that your MSB follow all of your Licensee/Principal's policies and procedures, the Principal/Licensee is generally responsible fulfilling vital Bank Secrecy Act requirements such as transaction monitoring, OFAC scanning and suspicious activity detection and reporting. In order to carry out these obligations, it is essential that the independent review process addresses your compliance with your Licensee's policies. Compliance with company policies and directives is also important information that your bank and regulators may want to verify.)

   ☐ *Yes*

   ☐ *No*

**Comments:**

**Follow-up:**

# AML Examinations

# AML Examinations

## IRS & State Banking Departments

1. **Complete the following table by noting the results of reviews by the IRS or State Banking Departments during the review period, and corrective actions taken or pending:**

   (Routine audits of your MSB may have been conducted by the IRS or State Banking Authorities. Use additional sheets if you need more room than the table provides.)

| DATE | EXAMINER | FINDINGS REQUIRING CORRECTIVE ACTION | CORRECTIVE ACTIONS TAKEN |
|---|---|---|---|
| | **IRS** | 1.<br>2.<br>3.<br>4.<br>5. | |
| | **State Banking Departments:**<br>**1.**__________<br>**2.**__________<br>**3.**__________<br>**4.**__________<br>**5.**__________ | 1.<br>2.<br>3.<br>4.<br>5. | |

## Licensees (Principals) & Banks

**2. Complete the following table by noting the results of reviews by your Licensee or Bank during the review period, and corrective actions taken or pending:**

(Routine audits of your MSB may have been conducted by the your Licensee or your Bank. Use additional sheets if you need more room than the table provides.)

| DATE | EXAMINER | FINDINGS REQUIRING CORRECTIVE ACTION | CORRECTIVE ACTIONS TAKEN |
|---|---|---|---|
| | **Licensee(s):**<br>**1.**__________<br>**2.**__________<br>**3.**__________<br>**4.**__________<br>**5.**__________ | 1.<br>2.<br>3.<br>4.<br>5. | |
| | **Banks**<br>**1.**__________<br>**2.**__________<br>**3.**__________<br>**4.**__________<br>**5.**__________ | 1.<br>2.<br>3.<br>4.<br>5. | |

# Appendix

# Appendix

## Guidance for Obtaining Banking Services

This guidance was issued by FinCEN on April 26, 2005. It contains information pertinent to your MSB obtaining banking services or maintaining the services it already has with your bank. Banks often misunderstand the nature of the money services business. It is therefore extremely important for you to ensure that your BSA compliance program is in good order and that your independent review is thorough and complete. This will ensure that your bank is comfortable carrying your account from its own risk prospective.

---

**Obtaining Banking Services – Basic Information Concerning the Money Services Business and Account Activity**

Banking organizations have been instructed, at a minimum, to take the following steps when determining whether to open or maintain an account for a money services business:

- ✓ Obtain basic identifying information about the money services business through the application of their Customer Identification Program;[1]
- ✓ Confirm FinCEN registration, if required;
- ✓ Confirm compliance with state or local licensing requirements, if applicable;
- ✓ Confirm agent status, if applicable; and,
- ✓ Conduct basic risk assessment to determine the level of risk associated with the account to solicit additional information, as deemed necessary.

A money services business should be prepared to provide this information to its banking organization when seeking to open an account or when requested to do so by its banking organization for purposes of maintaining an existing account relationship. Registration with FinCEN, if required, and compliance with any state licensing requirements represent the most basic of compliance obligations for money services businesses; a money services business operating in contravention of registration or licensing requirements would be violating Federal and possibly state laws.[2] As a result, banking organizations will require confirmation of a money services business's registration and licensing status prior to opening an account.

The extent to which a banking organization will seek additional information from a money services business beyond the minimums outlined above will be dictated by the banking organization's assessment of the level of risk posed by the individual customer. Care has been taken to remind the banking industry that not all money services businesses pose the same level of risk, and that not all money services businesses will always require additional due diligence. In some cases, the amount of additional customer due diligence performed by a banking organization will be negligible. In other situations, the additional due diligence performed will be extensive.

Like other financial institutions subject to the Bank Secrecy Act, money services businesses must assess the risks of their operations as a step in developing effective anti-money laundering programs. Money services businesses seeking to obtain or maintain account relationships with banking organizations should be prepared to provide information or explanation to their banking organizations about the risks associated with the services offered, the customer base, the markets served, and the locations of the money services business.

Such information may be very simple for many small money services businesses operating in local areas with limited products, in contrast with sophisticated, global money services businesses. Accordingly, money services businesses should be prepared to provide and explain to their banking organizations certain basic operational information:

1. **Types of products and services offered by the money services business**

   A money services business should help its banking organization understand:

   - ✓ The categories of services engaged in by the particular money service business;
   - ✓ Whether the money service business is a "principal" (with a fleet of agents) or an agent of

another money services business;
- ✓ Whether the money services business is new or an established operation; and,
- ✓ Whether or not money services represent a primary or ancillary aspect of the business (such as a grocery store that derives a small fraction of its overall revenue from cashing checks).

2. **Location(s) and Market(s) served by the money services business**

A money services business should help its banking organization understand:

- ✓ The markets it targets;
- ✓ The locations it serves;
- ✓ Whether it offers international services; and,
- ✓ Whether it caters exclusively to local residents.

3. **Anticipated account activity**

A money services business should help its banking organization understand:

- ✓ The services the business intends to use, such as currency deposits or withdrawals, check deposits, or funds transfers;
- ✓ The branch locations the business intends to use;
- ✓ Estimated transaction amounts; and,
- ✓ Any external or seasonal factors that may impact expected transactions.

4. **Purpose for the account**

A money services business should be prepared to explain to its banking organization the purposes for which its accounts would be used. For example, a money transmitter might require a bank account to remit funds to its principal U.S. clearing account or may intend to use the account to remit funds cross-border to foreign-based agents.

Finally, banking organizations have been advised to take additional steps in circumstances where, based on the collection of the information described above, heightened risk has been identified. Once again, care has been taken to explain that these additional steps are not appropriate in all cases and should not be considered the standard to be applied to all money services business accounts. Money services businesses should nonetheless be prepared to provide additional information to banking organizations, including details into the operation of their business and their anti-money laundering program. Such additional information could include –

- ✓ The money services business's anti-money laundering program;[3]
- ✓ The results of the money services business's independent testing of its anti-money laundering program;[4]
- ✓ Review list of agents, including locations, within or outside the United States, that will be receiving services directly or indirectly through the money services business account;
- ✓ Written procedures for the operation of the money services business;
- ✓ Written agent management and termination practices for the money services business; or,
- ✓ Written employee screening practices for the money services business.

Given the diversity of the money services business industry, and the directive in US regulations to apply the requirements of the Bank Secrecy Act on a risk-assessed basis, the extent and content of information identified above will vary markedly.

---

[1] Banking organizations are required to implement a Customer Identification Program.

[2] In addition to violating the FinCEN registration regulation, which can result in both civil and criminal penalties, failure to register with FinCEN is a violation of 18 U.S.C. 1960. See U.S. v. Uddin, No. 04-CR-80192 (E.D.Mich. April 11, 2005). Under certain circumstances, failure to obtain a required state license to operate a money services business can also result in a violation

of 18 U.S.C. 1960. See U.S. v. Velastegui, 199 F.3d 590 (2nd Cir. 1999).

[3] FinCEN's regulations require money services businesses to establish anti-money laundering programs tailored to their operations and the risks posed. 31 CFR 103.125. For example, the anti-money laundering program of a small money services business involved solely in the transmission of funds in small amounts will differ dramatically from the global money services business with both domestic and foreign agents.

[4] FinCEN's regulations do not require money services businesses to retain outside auditors to conduct the independent test of an anti-money laundering program. 31 CFR 103.125; 67 Fed. Reg. 21114 (Apr. 29, 2002) at 21115. This is especially important for small money services businesses that may not have the ability to retain an outside auditing firm.

## Conducting a Risk Assessment

Banks will naturally perform their own risk assessment on your business. A bank's assessment will consider the following items, and therefore, your own assessment should mirror what the banks are looking at:

**Types of products and services offered by the money services business**

In order to properly assess risks, banking organizations will seek to know the categories of money services engaged in by the your MSB. Relevant considerations will include whether or not your money services business is a new or established operation, and whether or not money services are your primary or ancillary business (such as a grocery store that derives a small fraction of its overall revenue from cashing checks).

**Location(s) and market(s) served by the money services business**

Money laundering risks within a money services business can vary widely depending on the locations, customer bases, and markets served by your money services business. Relevant considerations for banks will include whether markets served are:

- Domestic;
- International; or,
- Whether services are targeted to local residents or broad markets.

For example, a convenience store that only cashes payroll checks generally presents lower money laundering risks than a check casher that cashes any type of third-party check or cashes checks for commercial enterprises (which generally involve larger amounts).

**Anticipated account activity**

Banking organizations will seek to ascertain the expected services that your money services business will use, such as currency deposits or withdrawals check deposits, or funds transfers. For example, a money services business may operate out of one location and use one branch of the banking organization, or may have several agents making deposits at multiple branches throughout the banking organization's network. Banking organizations will want to have a sense of expected transaction amounts

**Purpose of the account**

Banking organizations will want to understand the purpose of the account for your money services business. For example, a money transmitter might require the bank account to remit funds to its principal U.S. clearing account or, may use the account to remit funds cross-border to foreign-based agents.

- Risk Assessment Items - **Indications of LOWER RISK**- Your MSB:
  - Primarily markets to customers that conduct routine transactions with moderate frequency in low amounts;
  - Offers only a single line of money services business product (for example, only check cashing or only currency exchanges);
  - Is a check casher that does not accept out of state checks;
  - Is a check casher that does not accept third-party checks or only cashes payroll or government checks;
  - Is an established business with an operating history;
  - Only provides services such as check cashing to local residents;
  - Is a money transmitter that only remits funds to domestic entities; or,
  - Only facilitates domestic bill payments.

- Risk Assessment Items - **Indications of LOWER RISK**- Your MSB:
  - Allows customers to conduct higher-amount transactions with moderate to high frequency; offers multiple types of money services products;
  - Is a check casher that cashes any third-party check or cashes checks for commercial businesses;
  - Is a money transmitter that offers only, or specializes in, cross-border transactions, particularly to jurisdictions posing heightened risk for money laundering or the financing of terrorism or to countries identified as having weak anti-money laundering controls;
  - Is a currency dealer or exchanger for currencies of jurisdictions posing heightened risk for money laundering or the financing of terrorism or countries identified as having weak anti-money laundering

controls;

- Is a new business without an established operating history; or,
- Is located in an area designated as a High Risk Money Laundering and Related Financial Crimes Area or a High-Intensity Drug Trafficking Area.

## US High Risk Locations

The areas depicted on the map below are considered High Intensity Drug Trafficking Areas (HIDTAs). HIDTA-designated counties comprise approximately 13 percent of U.S. counties, they are present in 43 states, Puerto Rico, the U.S. Virgin Islands and the District of Columbia. Your independent review should take note that you have reviewed these areas in relation to your business and that your MSB's controls are sufficient to deal with the heightened risks posed by doing business in these locales.

The map below depicts the areas considered to be High Intensity Financial Crimes Areas (HIFCAs). As with HIDTAs, your independent review should take note that you have reviewed these areas in relation to your business and that your MSB's controls are sufficient to deal with the heightened risks posed by doing business in these locales.

**For County names, see table below**

| **CA Northern District** | **CA Southern District** | **Southwest Border** | **Chicago** | **New York** | **Puerto Rico** | **South Florida** |
|---|---|---|---|---|---|---|
| Counties | Counties | Counties | Counties | Counties | Counties | Counties |
| Monterey<br>Humboldt<br>Mendocino<br>Lake<br>Sonoma<br>Napa<br>Marin<br>Contra Costa<br>San Francisco San Mateo Alameda<br>Santa Cruz<br>San Benito<br>Monterey<br>Del Norte | Los Angeles<br>Orange Riverside<br>San Bernardino<br>San Luis Obispo<br>Santa Barbara<br>Ventura | Arizona - All Counties<br>Texas - Counties bordering and adjacent to those bordering the US-Mexico border*<br><br>***See map below** | Cook<br>McHenry<br>Dupage<br>Lake<br>Will<br>Kane | New York - All Counties<br>New Jersey - All Counties | Puerto Rico - All Areas<br>U.S. Virgin Isles - All Areas | Broward<br>Miami-Dade<br>Indian River<br>Martin Monroe<br>Okeechobee<br>Palm Beach St Lucie |

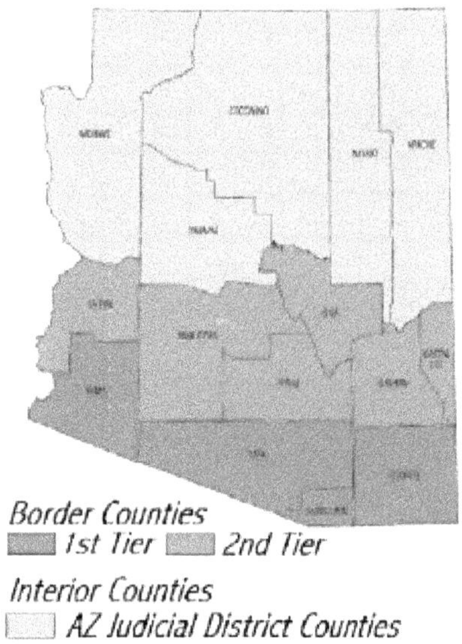
Border Counties
1st Tier
2nd Tier
Interior Counties
AZ Judicial District Counties

**TEXAS HIFCA**

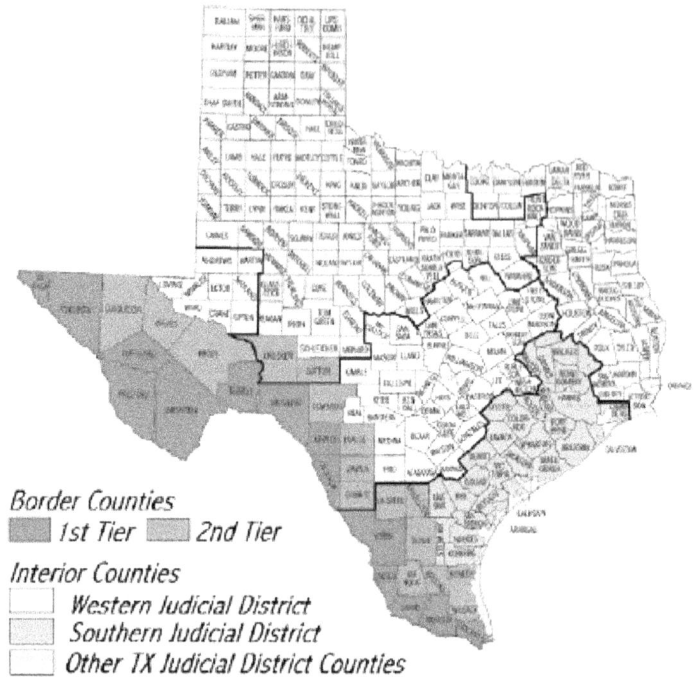
Border Counties
1st Tier
2nd Tier
Interior Counties
Western Judicial District
Southern Judicial District
Other TX Judicial District Counties

## Voluntary Information Sharing

Section 314(b) of the USA PATRIOT Act of 2001 allows certain financial institutions, after providing notice to FinCEN, to voluntarily share information with each other for the purpose of identifying and, where appropriate, reporting possible money laundering or terrorist financing under protection of legal safe harbor.[1]

Banks and money services businesses can utilize Section 314(b) information sharing to work together to identify money laundering and terrorist financing. **While participation in the 314(b) information sharing program is voluntary, FinCEN encourages banking organizations and their money services business customers to consider how voluntary information sharing could enable each institution to more effectively discharge its anti-money laundering and suspicious activity monitoring obligation.**

---

[1] Section 314(b) of the USA PATRIOT Act, as implemented by 31 CFR 103.110, establishes a safe harbor from liability for a financial institution or association of financial institutions that voluntarily chooses to share information with other financial institutions for the purpose of identifying and, where appropriate, reporting money laundering or terrorist activity. To avail itself of the 314(b) safe harbor, a financial institution must comply with the requirements of the implementing regulation, 31 CFR 103.110, including notice to FinCEN, verification that the other financial institution has submitted the requisite notice, and restrictions on the use and security of information shared. The safe harbor afforded by Section 314(b) is only available to financial institutions that are required to implement an anti-money laundering program, which includes banks regulated by a federal functional regulator (see 31 CFR 103.120) and money services businesses (see 31 CFR 103.125). For additional information on the 314(b) voluntary information sharing program, or to submit a notice to FinCEN to share information voluntarily, please refer to http://www.fincen.gov/.

## Additional Resources

FinCEN has made comprehensive resources available to money services businesses, free of charge, that provide information about compliance with the Bank Secrecy Act and explain how money services businesses can prevent money laundering.

FinCEN has established a web site, http://www.msb.gov dedicated to money services business regulations and guidance, such as FinCEN Rulings and answers to frequently asked questions.

Free, easy-to-understand educational materials include:

- ✓ "Quick Reference Guide to Bank Secrecy Act Requirements for Money Services Businesses"
- ✓ "Guide to Money Laundering Prevention"
- ✓ Posters and "Take One" cards, available in multiple languages and bi-lingual versions, to inform money services business customers about Bank Secrecy Act requirements and help customers understand why the business must ask for personal information.
- ✓ Videos and CD-ROMs, in English and Spanish, with case studies designed to educate money services business employees about the Bank Secrecy Act requirements.

Money services businesses can obtain these free educational materials by:

- Submitting an online order form through http://www.msb.gov/ (fastest option)
- Printing an order form from http://www.msb.gov/ and **faxing to 1-800-773-8356**
- Mailing to:

  **Money Services Business Program Office**
  **P.O. Box 39**
  **Vienna, VA 22183**
- Phoning an order to 1-800-386-6329

Additional help and information can be found from contacting the following sources:

- ✓ **For questions concerning Bank Secrecy Act requirements, contact FinCEN's Regulatory Helpline at 800-949-2732.**
- ✓ **To report suspicious activity that may be related to terrorist financing or ongoing money laundering schemes, contact FinCEN's Financial Institutions Hotline at (866) 556-3974.**
- ✓ Money Transmitter Regulators Association (http://www.mtra.web/) - the association of state regulators of the money transmitter industry.
- ✓ National Money Transmitters Association (http://www.nmta.us), or by phone at **(516) 829-2742**

State regulatory agencies and banking departments responsible for MSB registration and examination are the best source for guidance on how to comply with the specific requirements for each state. A contact list for the states' agencies can be found at the following web site:

http://www.msb.gov/pdf/msbstatecontactsfinal.pdf

www.ingramcontent.com/pod-product-compliance
Ingram Content Group UK Ltd.
Pitfield, Milton Keynes, MK11 3LW, UK
UKHW051508290926
15471UKWH00008B/1496

9 780615 23992